Papillon

Monsieur Butterfly

by Joyce Markovics

Consultant: Susi Gleffe
Past President of the Papillon Club of America

PUBLISHING

New York, New York

Publisher: Kenn Goin
Editorial Director: Adam Siegel
Creative Director: Spencer Brinker
Original Design: Dawn Beard Creative
Photo Researcher: Amy Dunleavy

Library of Congress Cataloging-in-Publication Data

Markovics, Joyce L.
 Papillon : monsieur butterfly / by Joyce Markovics ; consultant, Susi Gleffe.
    p. cm. — (Little dogs rock II)
 Includes bibliographical references and index.
 ISBN-13: 978-1-936088-17-1 (lib. bdg.)
 ISBN-10: 1-936088-17-7 (lib. bdg.)
 1. Papillon dog—Juvenile literature. I. Title.
 SF429.P2M37 2011
 636.76—dc22

                          2010016109

For more information, write to Bearport Publishing Company, Inc., 101 Fifth Avenue, Suite 6R, New York, New York 10003. Printed in the United States of America in North Mankato, Minnesota.

072010
042110CGF

10 9 8 7 6 5 4 3 2 1

Contents

Becoming Friends

People who lived near Debby Cantlon in View Ridge, Washington, knew that she enjoyed taking care of animals. So it was no surprise when someone called to ask if she would take care of an **orphaned** baby squirrel. Debby quickly said yes—even though it was a busy time for her. Debby's little dog, **Mademoiselle** Giselle (jiz-EL), was getting ready to have a **litter** of papillon (*pa*-pee-YAWN) puppies.

Debby planned on releasing the squirrel back into the wild after he was fully grown.

The tiny squirrel's name was Finnegan. He was about one week old when he came to live with Debby and her little fluffy dog. Debby wasn't sure, however, how Giselle would react to the baby squirrel. So she placed Finnegan in a small cage far from the tiny dog. Giselle then did something totally unexpected. She tugged the cage until it was next to her dog bed. Would the two animals become friends?

Papillons are known for being outgoing and friendly toward other animals— even cats.

▲ **Finnegan and Mademoiselle Giselle**

A Squirrel-Pup

Worried that the animals might not get along, Debby pushed Finnegan's cage back to its original spot. Once again, Giselle dragged the cage to her bedside. Debby knew then that Giselle wanted to care for the baby squirrel. So Debby let Finnegan out of his cage.

▲ **Without a mother, Finnegan could not care for himself. Debby fed the little squirrel using a small bottle.**

A few days later, Giselle gave birth to her babies. She was a great mother to her pups—and to one bushy-tailed squirrel! Giselle treated Finnegan as one of her own. She encouraged him to **nurse**. She even let the baby squirrel sleep with her puppies. Finnegan had found a new home, a new mom, and five new brothers and sisters.

Finnegan enjoyed snuggling with Giselle's puppies.

Puppies nurse, or drink their mother's milk, for up to eight weeks.

Portrait of a Pooch

Giselle's friendly and loving personality is one reason papillons have been **bred** for hundreds of years. In the 1500s, papillons were known as **dwarf**, or toy, spaniels. They were the prized pets of **noble** families in France, Spain, and Italy.

Dwarf spaniels were first bred in France, Spain, and Italy.

In the 1500s, an Italian artist ▶ named Titian (TISH-uhn) created many paintings of dwarf spaniels, including this one. He painted the dogs so frequently that they became known as "Titian spaniels."

At that time, dwarf spaniels were larger than they are today, but they were still small enough to sit comfortably on an owner's lap. They also had large, furry ears that dropped down. Well-known artists of the time would often paint portraits of noble families with their beloved pets.

A painting of a child named Clarissa and her pet spaniel by the artist Titian

The word *spaniel* means "dog of Spain" in Spanish, but spaniels were bred throughout Europe. Spaniels are small to medium-size dogs used for hunting and as companions.

Butterfly Dogs

Over time, dwarf spaniels became popular with noble families across Europe. During the 1700s and 1800s, however, the French wanted to change the way the little dogs looked. They bred the little spaniels so that they would have more delicate bones and large, furry ears that pointed up instead of down.

◀ The elegant papillon was the favorite pet of many French rulers, including Louis XIV (14), shown here seated in a chair.

◀ Today, some papillons still have ears that lay flat against their heads like the earlier dwarf spaniels. The dogs are called *phalenes*, which is the French word for "moths."

Marie Antoinette, who was Queen of France from 1774 to 1793, is believed to have owned and often carried papillons around with her.

The French didn't just change the way the little dogs looked. They also gave them a new name—papillon. This French word means "butterfly." The dogs were given this name because their huge, long-haired ears are shaped like butterfly wings. In addition, the markings on their faces often look like the body of a butterfly.

▲ The papillon's ears are light and delicate, much like a butterfly's wings.

Small and Smart

Today, papillons are popular all over the world, especially in the United States. People enjoy them because they are small, friendly—and very smart! What they lack in size, they make up for in brains.

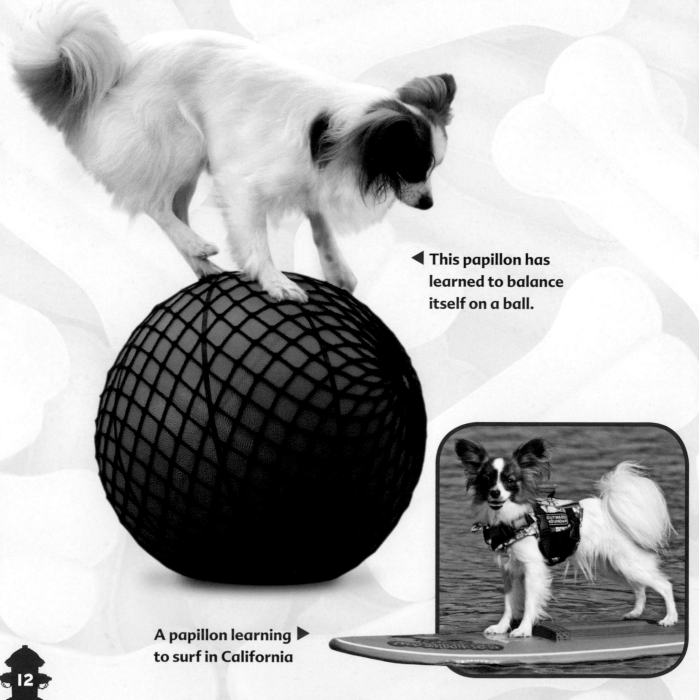

◀ **This papillon has learned to balance itself on a ball.**

A papillon learning ▶ to surf in California

Dr. Stanley Coren, a **psychologist** and dog trainer, studied more than 100 dog **breeds**. He rated the dogs on how well they were able to carry out **commands** and solve problems. Then he placed them in order according to their intelligence. The papillon was ranked as the eighth smartest breed.

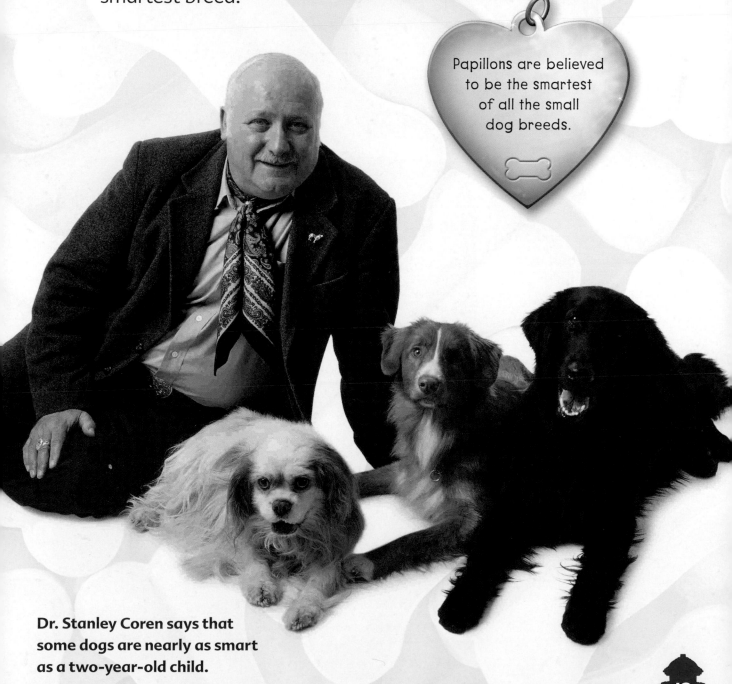

Papillons are believed to be the smartest of all the small dog breeds.

Dr. Stanley Coren says that some dogs are nearly as smart as a two-year-old child.

Very Obedient

Because of their intelligence, papillons are fast learners. It doesn't take long for owners to teach their clever dogs how to follow commands such as "sit," "stay," and "lie down." As a result, the little dogs are very good at **obedience trials**, or tests. During an obedience trial, a **handler** gives his or her dog a command. The dog receives points for how well it obeys its handler. Papillons often get top scores at these trials.

This papillon has ▶ learned to stand on two legs for its owner.

Papillons are one of the top five breeds in obedience training.

Some papillons are also taught to compete in **agility** contests. At these events, owners use their voices or hand signals to direct their dogs through an **obstacle course**. The papillons must dart through tunnels, leap over objects, and weave in and out of poles.

▲ Although papillons are very athletic, they are also happy to stay home and curl up on a warm lap.

◀ During an agility contest, a papillon is timed as it runs and jumps through a special course.

A Great Roommate

Papillons love to be around people. However, that also means they get sad when they are left alone. Luckily, the furry dog's small size makes it easy for an owner to carry the pet around town. Papillons easily fit into a bag or a large purse. So even when owners are away from home, they can be with their little friends.

▲ Papillons are happy to travel with their owners wherever they go.

Papillons are also easy to live with because of their small size. They don't need a lot of space to run around in or much exercise. Living in a small apartment or a big house makes no difference to these furry bundles. Like most dogs, however, they should be walked at least twice a day.

Although papillons don't need a lot of exercise, they enjoy spending time taking a walk with their owners.

Coats and Care

Along with regular exercise, papillons need to be brushed about twice a week. However, unlike other dogs with a lot of hair, papillons have **coats** that are easy to care for. That's because their fur is silky and does not **tangle** easily.

It's a good idea to ▶ start brushing a papillon while it is still a puppy so that it gets used to being groomed by the time it is an adult.

The long, soft hair on a papillon's tail is known as a **plume** because it looks like a large cluster of bird feathers.

A papillon with an ▶ elegant tail plume

18

Papillons' coats come in many colors. Most are white with patches of other colors, including black, brown, red, or tan. It is also common for papillons to have a strip of white fur down the middle of their faces.

A black and a reddish-brown papillon

◄ **Papillons often clean themselves the same way as a cat—by licking their paws and then washing their faces.**

Staying Healthy

Besides helping papillons look their best, owners also need to make sure their dogs feel their best. A papillon that is properly cared for can live a long, happy life. Part of caring for a papillon means taking it to a **veterinarian** to get regular medical checkups.

◀ Just like people, papillons need medical checkups to make sure they are healthy. A veterinarian is checking Spencer's teeth to make sure they are clean and strong.

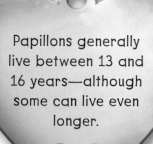

Papillons generally live between 13 and 16 years—although some can live even longer.

▲ A veterinarian is listening to Isabella's heart.

Papillon owners also need to make sure the little dogs don't hurt themselves. Papillons, especially puppies, love to jump off tall furniture. One papillon owner saw her dog jump from her bed to the top of a dresser. This can be dangerous for very small papillons or puppies because they have delicate bones that break easily. One way owners can help prevent broken bones is by making sure the dogs don't play on furniture.

A puppy that jumps down or falls from a tall chair or bed can hurt itself. So it's important for papillon owners to keep an eye on their pets.

Puppies

A newborn papillon puppy is so small it can easily fit into the palm of a person's hand. A papillon litter can be as small as one puppy. However, most papillon mothers have between two and four babies at a time. Like all kinds of puppies, they cannot care for themselves. They need to be fed and cleaned by their mother. A mother dog nurses her babies with milk from her body. She licks them with her tongue to keep them clean.

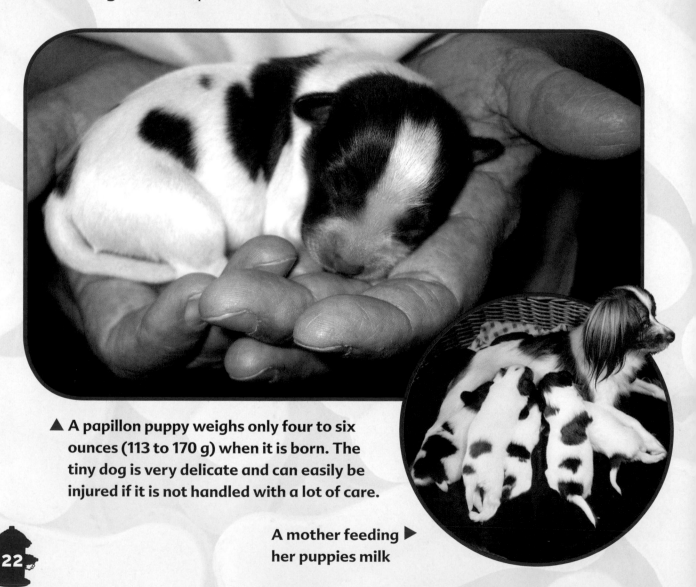

▲ A papillon puppy weighs only four to six ounces (113 to 170 g) when it is born. The tiny dog is very delicate and can easily be injured if it is not handled with a lot of care.

A mother feeding ▶ her puppies milk

Larger kinds of puppies, such as German shepherds or collies, are usually ready to leave their mother at the age of 8 weeks. Papillon puppies, however, need a few more weeks to build up their strength. When they are about 12 weeks old, they are strong enough to leave their mother and become part of a human family.

Children must be taught to be gentle when playing with papillon puppies. If they aren't, they may break the puppies' delicate bones.

When fully grown, papillons are still small. Most are under one foot (30 cm) tall at the shoulder and weigh about four to nine pounds (2 to 4 kg)—less than most pet cats.

Helping Out

Most puppies grow up as pets in homes with human families. Some, however, receive special training to help people with **disabilities**. These dogs become **service dogs**. They help people such as Debi Davis, a dog trainer who lost her legs and now uses a wheelchair to get around. "Papillons make excellent service dogs," Debi says. The little dogs love to spend all day helping their owners. They are also quick to learn new tasks.

Service dogs are taught to help people who cannot see or hear, or who have mental or physical disabilities. A special trainer teaches a service dog how to do everything from guiding a person across the street to turning a light switch on or off.

▼ **Debi and her service dog Peek**

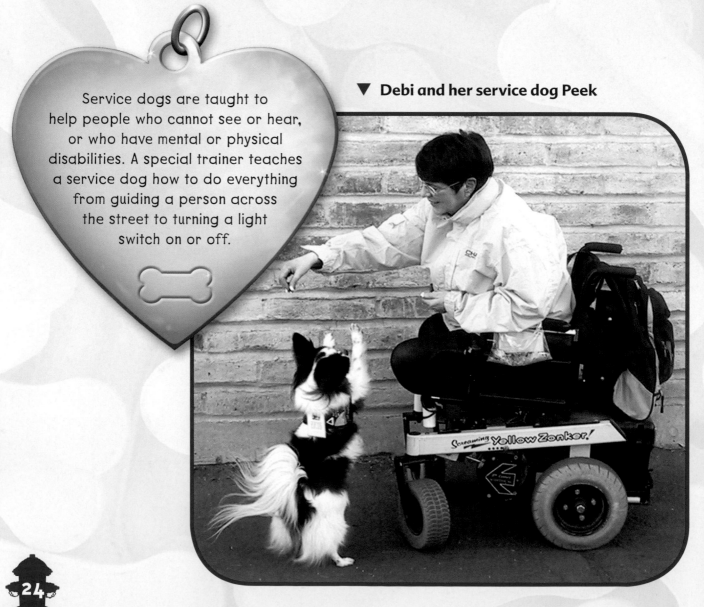

Debi's service dog—a papillon named Peek—helps out with many daily chores. For example, making the bed is a snap for Debi with Peek by her side. He uses his mouth to pull up the bedsheets and drag the pillows into place. Peek also helps out with the laundry. He grabs clean clothes from the dryer. After Debi folds them, he puts them away in drawers.

▲ **Peek climbs into the dryer and pulls out the clean clothes for Debi.**

A Forever Friend

Just like Peek, Piper is also a service dog. The eight-pound (4-kg) papillon works for Karen Shirk. Karen has a disease that makes it hard for her to breathe. Luckily, Piper **senses** when Karen is going to have an attack that could cause her to stop breathing. The little dog barks and jumps up and down, letting Karen know that she should take medicine to stop the attack.

Karen and Piper

Karen started an organization called 4 Paws for Ability to help people with disabilities—especially children—find service dogs. Sometimes the dogs she finds and trains are papillons, which shouldn't come as a big surprise. After all, papillons aren't just great pets and companions. These tiny dogs with the huge butterfly ears can be lifesavers as well.

In 2009, Piper gave birth to two puppies. One of the puppies received training to become a service dog, just like her mother!

▲ Piper

Papillons at a Glance

Weight:	4–9 pounds (2–4 kg)
Height at Shoulder:	8–11 inches (20–28 cm)
Coat Hair:	Long, silky, and flowing, with fringed hair on the ears
Colors:	One main color, such as white, with patches of other colors, such as black, brown, red, or tan
Countries of Origin:	France, Spain, and Italy
Life Span:	About 13 to 16 years
Personality:	Alert, friendly, and intelligent

Best in Show

What makes a great papillon? Every owner knows that his or her dog is special. Judges in dog shows, however, look very carefully at a papillon's appearance and behavior. Here are some of the things they look for:

large ears with round tips are set near the back of the head; they may stand up or drop down

skull is small and has a round shape

tail is covered with a plume of long hair and arches over the body

eyes are dark and round

lips are tight, thin, and black

coat is white with patches of color; fur is long, flowing, and silky

Behavior: should be happy, alert, friendly, and not shy

Glossary

agility (uh-JIL-uh-tee) the ability to move fast and easily

bred (BRED) when dogs from specific breeds are mated to produce young with certain characteristics

breeds (BREEDZ) kinds of dogs

coats (KOHTS) the fur or hair on dogs or other animals

commands (kuh-MANDZ) orders given to a person or animal

disabilities (*diss*-uh-BILL-uh-teez) conditions that make it hard for a person to do everyday things such as walking, seeing, or hearing

dwarf (DWORF) a kind of animal that is smaller than usual

handler (HAND-lur) a person who trains and works with animals

litter (LIT-ur) a group of baby animals, such as puppies or kittens, that are born to the same mother at the same time

mademoiselle (*mad*-mwuh-ZEL) the French word for *Miss*

noble (NOH-buhl) a person of high rank

nurse (NURSS) to drink milk from one's mother

obedience trials (oh-BEE-dee-uhnss TRYE-uhlz) tests where dogs show how well they obey their owners

obstacle course (OB-stuh-kuhl KORSS) a path set up with objects, such as cones and poles, that a person or animal moves through

orphaned (OR-fuhnd) someone whose parents have died

plume (PLOOM) long, fluffy feathers

psychologist (sye-KOL-uh-jist) a person who studies people's minds and behavior

senses (SENS-iz) feels or is aware of something

service dogs (SUR-viss DAWGZ) dogs that are trained to do daily tasks for people with disabilities or who have health problems

tangle (TANG-uhl) to twist together or become knotted

veterinarian (*vet*-ur-uh-NER-ee-uhn) a doctor who takes care of dogs and other animals

Bibliography

Truex, F. Michael. *Papillon: A Comprehensive Guide to Owning and Caring for Your Dog.* Allenhurst, NJ: Kennel Club Books (2005).

Wood, Deborah. *A New Owner's Guide to Papillons.* Neptune City, NJ: T.F.H. Publications (2003).

www.akc.org/breeds/papillon (American Kennel Club)

www.papillonclub.org (Papillon Club of America)

Read More

Arden, Darlene. *Small Dogs, Big Hearts: A Guide to Caring for Your Little Dog.* Hoboken, NJ: Howell Book House (2006).

Hungerland, Jacklyn E. *Papillons: Everything About Purchase, Care, Nutrition, Behavior, and Training.* Hauppauge, NY: Barron's Educational Series (2003).

Learn More Online

To learn more about papillons, visit
www.bearportpublishing.com/LittleDogsRockII

Index

About the Author

Joyce Markovics is an editor, writer, and orchid collector. She lives with her husband, Adam, and an eel-shaped amphibian named Merrylegs. She hopes to get a furry pet in the near future to keep Merrylegs company.